In love with the Flame

IN LOVE WITH THE FLAME

Cover and illustrations via www.shutterstock.com

Art Director: Perri Farlow

First edition: November 2024

ISBN: 979-8-218-52883-6

Lighthouse Publishing

In love with the Flame

David Willard

LIGHTHOUSE
— PUBLISHING —

In the early mornings

she found time to read

and I would write

with the sun spilling light

across the bedroom floor

and my heart would sing

for the beautiful dream

that I was living with her.

I sure wouldn't call it subtle

the intensity of love

for in my heart lies the magnitude

of a thousand thundering storms.

In love I need to brace

for what I'm about to feel

a cyclone of emotions

with you the eye of the storm.

I'll be your sun

on the rainiest of days

if you'll be my moon

shining your light in the dark

and together we can share

the twilight sky.

I want to love you again

while I race to fall asleep

into a sea of dreams

and leave this world behind.

I want to wake up

with you by my side

a smile and a good morning kiss

and fall in love with you

all over again.

Let me take you away
from this imperfect reality
to a private inner place
where you rule a heart
that beats exclusively for you.

The cratered moon reminds me

that you don't need perfection

in order to be magical.

You carry your little flaws

in the most beautiful way

with a heart that glows

and an innocence that shines.

I want you to always be wondrous

like no other star in the sky

and, my love, I promise

you will always be beautiful.

One winter evening

in an art museum

I didn't notice the paintings

for I only had eyes

for this girl across the room.

Her brown eyes twinkled

a thousand different moments

of a life spent together,

a couple growing old,

her hand always in mine.

Before I could say hello

you had already captured me

and even to this day

I feel lost in you.

Who is this girl that gives me this feeling,

a feeling for which I'll never find the words,

a little piece of heaven that is mine,

your voice that softens like angels

and your words can perform miracles,

alone together in a paradise with you.

Love unlocks my heart

and out of the darkness

I open my eyes

to a world bleeding with colors,

a world that's been sleeping

inside of me

waiting for you

to provide the key.

My love, you lit a fire in me.

You kindled and created

a light bright enough

to illuminate dark corners

and pierce the night sky.

You've entered my heart

and like the moth

mesmerized by the light

I hope you are inspired

to come even closer

to continue loving me

and watching me burn.

When I hold you in my arms

I want you to bloom just for me

into a million different colors

and a thousand shades of love.

Your heart shines out like a beacon

that brightens the darkened sky

and I will keep on holding you

the way the night sky holds the moon.

YOUR TOUCH IS A CHEMISTRY

A FORMULA OF MAGIC

THAT LEAVES ME TREMBLING

FOREVER WANTING MORE

AFTER EVERY SINGLE TOUCH.

Tonight we set sail

across an ocean of love

with the midnight moon

painting our sails.

We'll sail a gentle breeze

while the waves lap our boat

and it doesn't matter

where we make port

because anywhere you are

will always be my home.

You came into my life

like a song, somehow,

I've always been humming

and you fit into my routine

like the glove my hand

has always been wanting.

Look how neatly you fell

into my life and made it

all so comfortable.

I'd climb the tallest mountain

to reach out and touch the moon.

I'd become the night sky

so I can hold her

tightly in my arms.

I'd become a shining star

to sleep alongslide her at night.

My moon,

come shine your light for me

one more time.

Late night strolls

through fields of clover

hidden spots

and secret gardens.

My darling, all I want

is for you to be my secret moon

to be the light in my night sky.

We seed our kisses

the world eclipses

and I fall deep inside of you.

I like you most when

it's 8am and you're having your coffee

in the oversized t-shirt you wore

to bed last night

with your hair all a mess

just trying to wake up.

You may not think so

but this is when I think you're perfect.

Saying "I love you"

just wasn't enough.

Then you took a knife

and carved your name

into my heart.

When water touches my lips

it's transformed into wine

and everything I touch

turns to gold.

It's not magic I possess

but the alchemy of love,

the ability to transform

my entire world

into a miracle.

What your love has shown me

is not what you can be

that I am not

but rather what I can

become.

Among a thousand stars

I'd choose your radiant light

and with that beautiful smile

I have the courage to fight

for a life I want with you

more than anything else

to share forever together

our feelings forever felt.

I barely left your side

those first couple weeks

tangled in kisses

and thoughts of forever.

The heart craves

to fall in love

but it doesn't have to be

with a specific person

for my heart's in love

with the quiet silence

of the early morning,

the way one laughs

together with friends,

the smell of a new book,

and rainy afternoons.

The heart craves to feel

what it means most

to be alive.

I may not have all the answers

but I have you

and I think that's enough.

I am the flame

that burns with the passion of love

an uncontrollable fire

as well as a warmth that nurtures.

To love me is to accept them both

the inner storm of fire

as well as the warm embrace it brings.

I'll write a poem

that breathes into life

a beautiful star

that I'll pluck from the sky

and hang in my heart

so I'm forever reminded

that just one little poem

can create something beautiful.

I seem to feel your presence

in everything around me,

in the stars overhead,

an early morning sunrise,

on rainy afternoons,

and in every passing smile.

Let me shower you with affection

and bathe you in the downpour of love

for how could you not expect me

to embrace the boundless storm

that thunders in my heart.

Before you I lived

with monsters in my mind

but when your love

poured its light

into a world full of shadows

you became my nightlight in the dark

keeping the monsters away.

Love is having someone

who has seen you after

you have just woken up,

who has heard you sing

all your made-up songs,

who knows all your

secrets and insecurities

and still loves you anyway.

"I love you" tells a story

of the first time we held hands

watching the setting sun

and realizing your beauty

could never be contained

by all the poetry in the world.

Love is a recollection

of these perfect moments

I've spent with you.

When I wake up
and kiss you good morning,
when I give you a hug
after a long day at work,
what I am saying is that
I choose you
that I accept you as you are
with your perfect little flaws.

We walk alongside the St. Johns river

the sunset dripping off our clothing

painting the world in shades of pink

before burying itself in the dancing waves.

Darling, what force do you possess over me

pulling me like a magnet towards you?

On evenings like these there exists

no force that can stop this attraction

that pulls me closer and closer to you.

Nobody in this world is perfect.

What really matters

is whether you're perfect

for each other.

You had your scars

just like I had mine.

Darling, let my love pass

through these scars

and heal your wounds.

I want to make you believe

in love once again.

Nobody in this world is perfect

but I think that we are perfect

for each other.

Haven't we all been told

that we can be

anything we want to be

but what I wanted

was to be yours.

Your love is a warm blanket

of safety and security

and the ironic thing about love

is the more vulnerable I become

the safer I will be.

I want to fall in love with you

so I can grow wings and fly.

With you I feel I can do

the extraordinary

the impossible.

Tonight I want to seed kisses in your soul

and watch them bloom

like no other star in the sky.

I want you to be beautiful

entirely for me

and hear all the ways

you feel about me

because, my love,

you've set my heart ablaze.

Today I felt like kissing you

a feeling that takes me

one step over a cliff.

Today I felt like hugging you

your celestial soul

a passionate heart.

Today I felt like whispering in your ear

that I want you forever.

In this world of intensity and fervor

I only want you.

No one ever told me

the most beautiful thing

in the world

is to wake up

next to the person you love.

If you be my moon

I'll be your ocean.

At dusk I'll wait

for your warm embrace

and I'll submerge your heart

in a sea of love.

Does it sound silly to say

that I couldn't write

before I met you?

But now that you've

taken my heart

and lit my world on fire

I find poetry

on every beam of light.

I've been dreaming of someone

to be the moon in my night sky

to pour their light

onto the darkened path

and even though the sun

may steal you away from me at dawn

I know you'll always

come back for me.

My love, I'll be waiting for you

in the twilight sky.

Sometimes when I kiss you

I can feel the earth move.

Sometimes when I look

into your deep brown eyes

I can see all of time.

Sometimes when you place

your hand in mine

I feel the greatest comfort.

If I could live

a thousand different lifetimes

I know I'd love you

in each and every one of them.

Love paints the way
I see the world
and I start to find beauty
in all the little things,
your funny quirks
your little flaws,
that make me love
exactly who you are.

I can't wait to spend every day with you.

To wake up next to you

play and push you around the bed

while you ask me

"how do you have so much energy this early!"

To be entwined in each other's arms.

The way I pull the curls of your hair

and watch them pop back into place.

The moments we kiss

when we pass each other in the hallway.

The movies that take all day to finish

because we find ourselves in bed again.

The late night walks we take together

and of course

the little fights in between.

David Willard

IF YOU'RE LUCKY ENOUGH

TO FIND SOMEONE BEAUTIFUL

MAKE SURE YOU TELL THEM SO

You wanted to learn to read poetry
the way I do
inspired by its love and passion.
I watched your lips move
as your mind read the words
and I wish I could go back
and watch those lips once again
silently dance with poetry.

When I first met you

you were an independent girl

so I let you lead

but you taught me

not how to follow

but how to live alongside you.

We made our way in the world

together.

I bathe in the warm light

of the fire that burns

deep within my heart

from a love that was ignited

with a first kiss

and a thousand days beside you.

With you

I want to chase

all my beautiful dreams.

I want to catch

every ray of the sun

and dress you up

in dazzling light.

I want to explore

everything beautiful about you

with your little flaws

eclipsed like a crescent moon.

Remember that night
lying on the beach
we stared at the stars
and kissed for hours?
You opened your heart
and I fell deep into you.

Falling in love with you

was like falling into

the warmest of dreams,

a gentle ocean

that rocks me sleep,

a moonlit path

to guide my way.

In love

I sometimes don't feel like myself.

I've given you all my little pieces

and when you leave

a piece of me goes missing.

I wear your love

like a warm blanket

and without you

I feel naked.

You leave the room

and in this empty space

I intensely feel your absence.

My love, I need you next to me

the same as I need air.

The stars in the night sky

are witness to how long

I've searched for you.

You ran through my heart

like a wildfire

setting everything ablaze.

I no longer need the stars

to find my way at night

because in you I've found

my moon

to illuminate my night sky.

I'm not really
a jealous person, but
I'm jealous of the coffee
that touches your lips

I'm jealous of the work
that demands your attention

I'm jealous of the clothes
that hold your body

I'm jealous of the covers
that keep you warm in bed

and I'm jealous of the stars
that watch over you at night.

Sometimes I wake

in the middle of the night

and look over and see

you lying next to me.

It's in these moments I know

my heart beats for you

as you lie there and dream.

My love, I wonder

does your heart also beat

for me?

She was the kind of girl

who could walk into a room

and steal the breath from your lungs.

Sometimes it's our fingers

that hold the most important conversations.

The way my fingers run down your back

under the sheets.

The way we hold hands

on our nightly walks.

The way I touch the back of your neck

while we watch a movie at night.

I often only need my fingers to tell you

that I desire you more than anything

in this world.

Look how perfectly

your hand fits in mine.

I stand above you

and you can't even kiss me

unless you're on tiptoe.

Look how perfectly

my arms wrap around you

as you hug my waist.

Together we may look

like two opposites

but look how perfectly

we fit together.

You may leave me tomorrow

but, darling, please,

tell me one more time

that you love me

and I promise

this time I'll be brave.

If we were to end tomorrow

and you sift through the ashes

of my broken heart

you would find that you

were what was inside.

From the moment

I first saw you

I knew you would be

worth the heartbreak.

My heart screams

that it's in love with you

and even with those scars

you still find a way

to unleash an endless love.

I've seen you cry

in tender moments

and I know your heart goes out

to those you help every day.

Can I tell you, my love,

that I hope your heart

remains forever soft.

I love your little flaws
that tell me a story
of exactly who you are.

In you I've found

something wild

and I want to run

alongside you

not to catch you

but so that we may

both be free.

When I dream of
kissing you,
when I think about
holding your hand,
I want to take
that little heart of yours
and keep it forever.

WE'VE GIVEN EACH OTHER

ALL THE LITTLE PIECES

OF OUR HEARTS.

TOO CLOSE NOW

TO EVER BE APART.

Who is this girl

whose eyes dance

to the playlist of my mind,

whose voice reverberates

to the deepest part of my soul.

It feels as if

we've already spent

a lifetime together,

our story already written

in the stars.

How could I not love you

for the rest of time.

I'm fascinated by your love

that spills all around me

a thousand different ways

a million bleeding colors

that paint my world

every color of the sun.

Darling, can we grow old together

watching a thousand sunsets,

walking through moonlit fields,

exploring foreign cities,

always hand in hand.

I want to grow old with you

and share these moments

for the rest of time.

You had a rare gift

to find me in the dark

and make me believe

I could be so much more.

I once bought a diamond

that twinkled in the light

but it wouldn't replicate

what I saw in your eyes.

You had this special ability

to fill my heart

with all the words

I never knew were there.

My love can be messy

for a passionate fire

burns within my heart

spilling over

in the form of

tulips and sunflowers,

moments beneath the sheets,

fights and arguments.

I'll never apologize

for its intensity

because in the fire

I feel most alive.

Love paints the way

I see the world

and I start to find beauty

in all the little things,

your funny quirks,

your little flaws,

that make me love

exactly who you are.

David Willard

WHAT I FOUND IN YOU

WERE ALL THE THINGS

I DIDN'T KNOW

I WAS SEARCHING FOR.

I don't want perfect

for love is complex

when engulfed in passion

and in this fire that burns

I find ecstasy

in the beautiful chaos.

With every passing moment

that I spend with you

I become a little more sure

that anything is possible.

From your warm lips

I draw the moonlight.

A sip from this cup

and I'm intoxicated with you

a drunken feeling that lasts

but a lifetime.

I think about you

a thousand times a day

and today I feel that

I'm even more in love with you

than I was yesterday.

I tell you everything

my dreams, my feelings

and in this vulnerability

you imbue my world with hope.

When we are apart

I write poetry

to bring you closer to me.

My love, is there a better way

to tell you that

I miss you?

Our love is like

a collision of two galaxies

twirling and coalescing

where two hearts become one.

A new world is formed

something never seen before

a world created by love.

Even though the words

may hang in my throat

perhaps, darling,

the greatest expression of love

is the actions we take

as we make our way together

that tells the truest story of our love.

In your eyes

I can see all the stars

and I can feel your heart

spreading light

across the universe.

Darling, I only want

you to be my moon

to spread this light

and keep these nights

till the end of time.

Tell me all your secrets

so I may see your world

through your eyes

to know your past

and feel your pain.

I'll keep your little secrets

safely in my heart.

In our love

I give myself

entirely to you

and in this vulnerability

you have the power

to shatter me

but our love

is one that heals

and makes me stronger

than I ever was before.

Sometimes I sing songs with made-up lyrics

when we wake up in the early morning

because you're not really a morning person.

My love may be in a different language

but it still speaks the same message

that I love you.

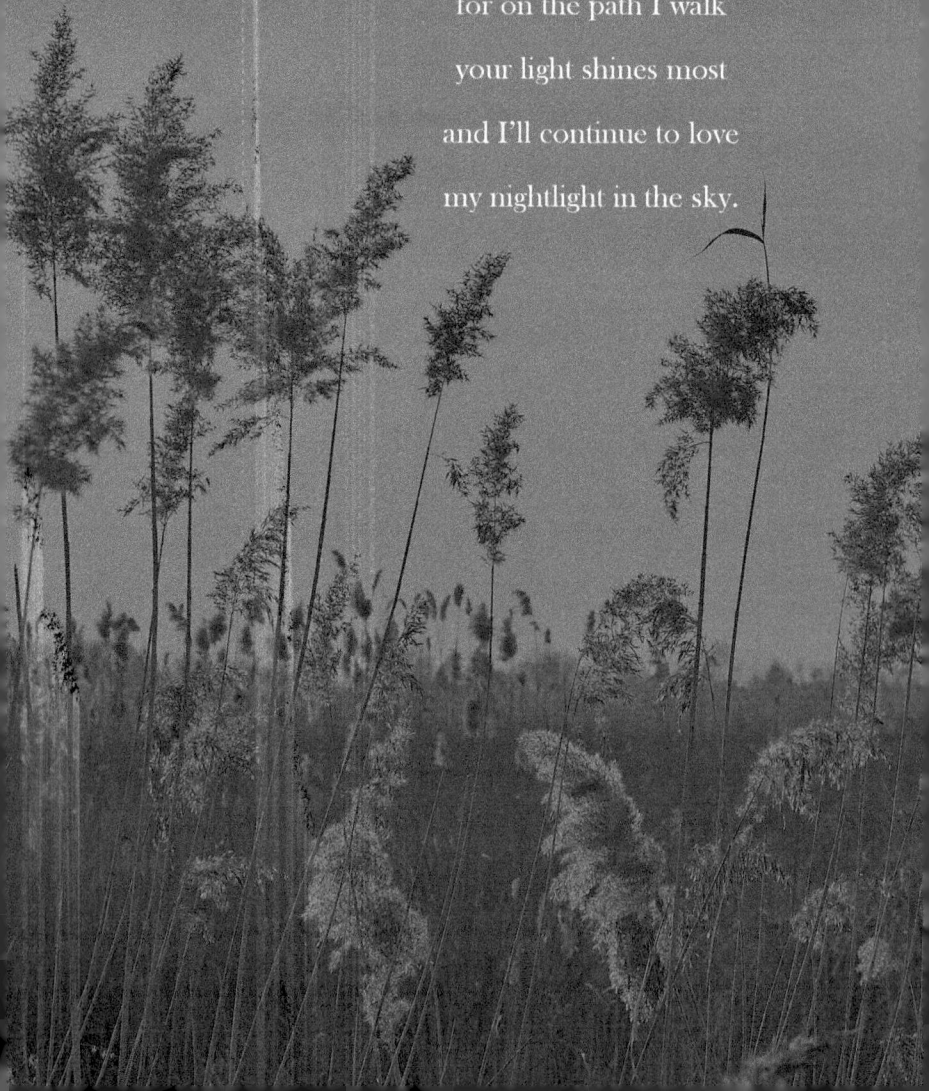

In your love I've found

my moon that shines

her eternal nightlight

painting the night sky

in deep midnight blue

for on the path I walk

your light shines most

and I'll continue to love

my nightlight in the sky.

You paint my heart

in hues of bliss

and remind me of love

with just a kiss.

In your warm embrace

is where I belong

while my heart sings

our beautiful song.

Poetry gives me the strength

to say the things

my heart wishes I would say.

My love, when you read this

know that I love you.

A goodnight kiss

brings a wave of peace

before falling into a dream

and a good morning smile

warms my heart

against the cool morning air.

My love, you wear my heart

around your neck

and to be honest

I think it looks good on you.

My heart waited like a seed

for you to be the water

that nourished it back to life

dreaming of the chance

to bloom in the sun

but staying awake at night

just to see the moon.

Lying there next to you

all my worries

are far away.

We chase our dreams

among the stars at night

until the light of dawn

kisses our faces

lying there next to you.

For all these passing years

I've carried a smoldering ember

deep inside my chest

in hopes that one day

you'd be brave enough

to search for me

to find that smoldering ember

and with warm words

breathe it back to life.

My love, I've been waiting

to rekindle this fire of love

that burns as bright as the sun.

When I hold you in my arms

your love shines outward

like a thousand twinkling stars.

It's in these moments

I feel I have everything.

Maybe this is paradise

for I can't help but wonder

at the magic that you are.

You sit at the pinnacle

of a terrifying beauty

daring and threatening

to engulf the hearts

of any who'd attempt

to tame your passion.

An earthquake of feeling

brings a tsunami of love

sweeping away lovers

in your beautiful chaos.

I want to be more

than just a shooting star

screaming across the night sky

a temporary brilliance

and then forgotten.

No, I want to love

like the sun wants to shine,

to always be the gentle embrace

that provides eternal warmth.

If you remember me for anything

I hope it's the passion with which I love

for I know my love isn't easy.

You've had my love on the sunniest of days

and listened to the thunder of passing storms.

In love I give you all of myself

so while a cloud may block the light for a bit

behind it lies a love as bright as the sun.

You're the type of girl

that after all this time

can still put butterflies in my stomach

and make me feel like I'm seeing you

for the very first time all over again.

Don't feel afraid

of the thunder

heard in the distance

for deep in my heart

lies a building storm

set to unleash

a downpour of love.

Lay your hand on my chest
and feel the warmth of a fire
that burns entirely for you,
a flame that pours its light
into the dark between stars
and with it I'll fill the sky
with all my love for you.

I MAY BE A POET

BUT THAT DOESN'T MEAN

I HAVE ALL THE WORDS

TO DESCRIBE A LOVE

THAT'S IMPOSSIBLE TO CAPTURE.

I can't say it was surprising

that I fell in love with you,

with a deluge of feelings

that overflowed my boundaries

and submerged my heart.

No, I can't really say

that I'm all that surprised.

How do I keep my heart

from floating away

for I constantly fill it up

with all our little moments

and each and every smile.

Your hand holds the string

that's tethered to my heart.

My love, please don't let go.

Let me peel away

all your outer layers

till I arrive at the beating core

of a loving heart.

What I want you to see

is that in your raw vulnerability

I find you simply beautiful.

I had hidden a little place

where love had never grown

because I had yet to find

the perfect one.

When you came along

this secret hidden place

grew into a beautiful garden

with flowers that celebrate

the fact that I found you.

David Willard

My heart is reborn

with the rising sun

and no amount

of darkness

can keep my love

from finding you.

When our fingers interlock

and our bodies touch

my heart is lit up

like a thousand fireworks.

I hope we can keep this magic

for the rest of time.

What I want from you is easy.
I want those shimmering eyes
that twinkle in the sunlight,
I want that angelic voice
that sings to your favorite songs,
and I want that little heart of yours
to keep safely in my chest
while it fills the midnight sky
with its beautiful moonlight.

The sound of your voice

is a love song

I sing inside my head

the melody of which

I've memorized by heart.

I can't help but feel happy

that maybe your song

was written just for me.

You were brave enough

to take my hand

and dance in the flame

of a heart that burns

for no one but you.

Tonight I'll whisper to the moon

while the rest of the world sleeps

and while I bathe in the moonlight

I'll let her know that I finally found

a love worth keeping.

You grab me like the moon

grabs the sea at high tide

and you guide me to a height

I never thought possible.

A new life began

when you kindled the flame

that burns in my heart.

The me before you

heartbreak and tears

are forever gone

for nothing exists

the two of us don't share.

I don't know exactly when

you became my everything

but I do know that

your love has made me new.

Your love paints my world
in pastel watercolors
colors I may not always see
but I can constantly feel.
My heart is a canvas
painted with brilliant hues
curves and contrasts
that tell a beautiful story
of our life together.

David Willard

You see, if you told me

our story was ending

I'd ask that you let me

hold you in my arms,

give you one last kiss,

tell you I love you,

and that'll be our end

because what good is a story

without a little heartbreak.

Is there anyone
in this world
who can touch my heart
the way you have?

My love, take my hand

and we'll navigate the flames

that burn in my heart

bursting on impulse

spontaneous and raw

for deep in my heart

lies an unteachable love.

In your eyes I see

a twinkling reflection

with its own dream

of falling in love

with the moon.

A nighttime walk

to a secret garden,

the air filled with

the smell of honeysuckle

the damp dew grass

and the trickling sound

of the nearby brook.

On nights like this

I want to spend

just a little more forever

with you.

You make little mistakes
I dismiss with forgiveness.
Each and every fault
makes me smile with compassion
for our love is one
that nurtures and accepts
and in this imperfect love
we'll continue to flourish.

Do you think if I had met you

in maybe a different place

a different time

that I would've found

those countless sunsets

and tangled kisses

that I eventually found

in you?

Still after all this time

with one touch from you

the sparks ignite again

and I'm caught

in that starry-eyed gaze

and that smitten smile.

You have this way

of bringing me back

to the purely magical.

What I really want is

to pick you flowers

sing you a song

and give you a hug

just to see you

smile at me again

the way you just did.

You have stolen from me

my heart and soul

and, my love,

you can keep them

you beautiful bandit.

I dive below the surface
determined to explore
your shy and bashful heart.
I want to find your secret treasures
and capture all your wildest dreams
all just to get a glimpse
at the woman you really are.

A hug from you

warms like a fire

on a winter night

and your voice

sings like the siren

steering my heart

toward rocky shores.

The touch of your skin

sends electric sparks

deep down my spine

while the stars sparkle

in the blacks of your eyes.

David Willard

I FELL IN LOVE WITH YOU

UNDER THE WINTER SUN

AND STAYED WRAPPED UP

IN YOUR HUGS AND KISSES

WARM AS SUMMER.

Don't be afraid

of the scars you carry

for they tell a story

of where you've been

and where you might go.

And if you know me

then you should know

I love a good story.

Sometimes our hands say more

as we walk hand in hand

than do the words

of our conversations.

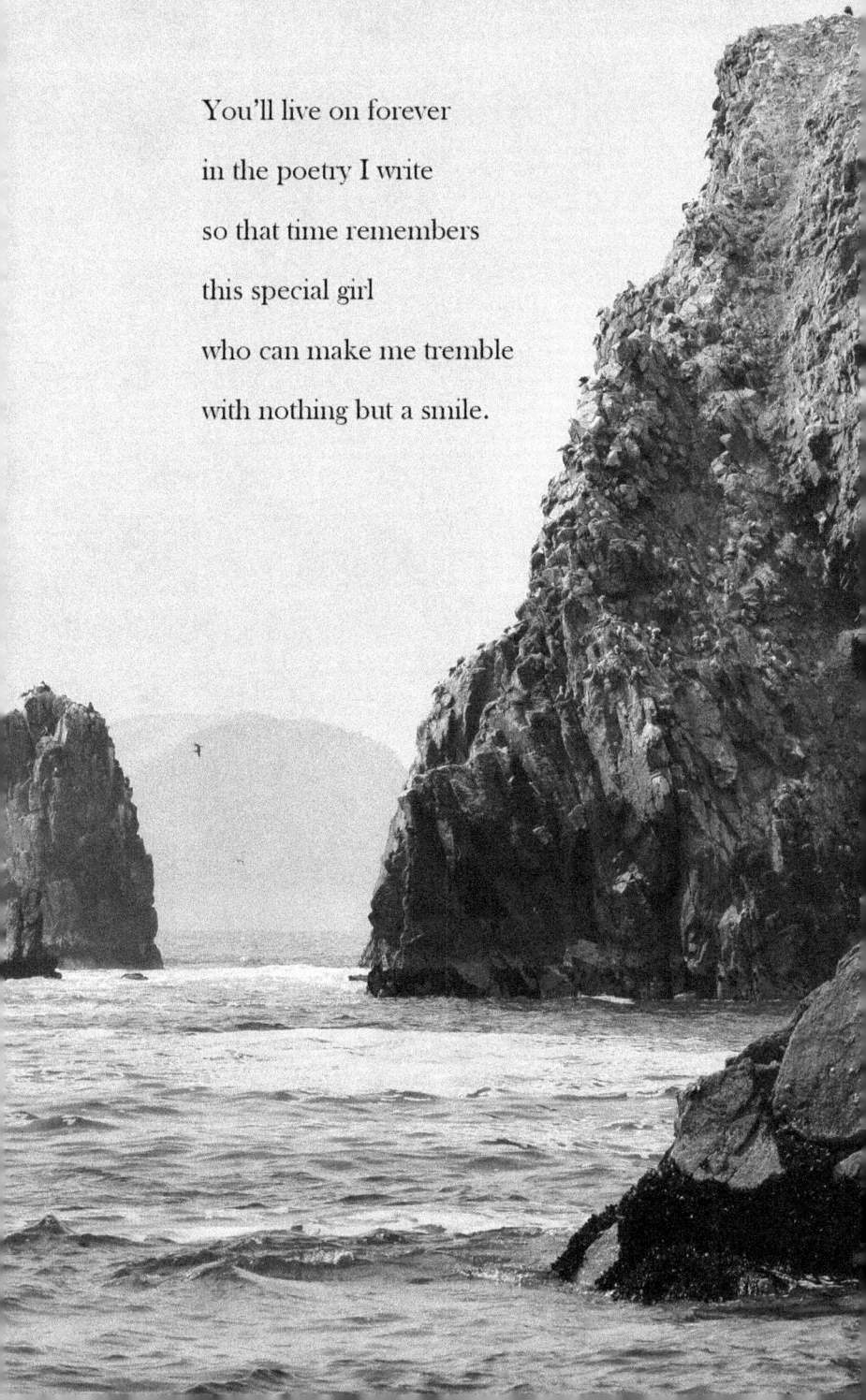

You'll live on forever

in the poetry I write

so that time remembers

this special girl

who can make me tremble

with nothing but a smile.

You came into my life

like a shooting star

screaming and blazing

your brilliant flames

right into my heart,

I just hope you stay a while.

I love your little quirks
just as much as I love
your superior qualities.
Darling, there's no need
to be hard on yourself
because I love all of the
woman you've become,
quirks, flaws, and all.

A mighty storm threatens

to tear apart the very fabric

of my beating heart.

Not out of anger or fear

but out of a love

that knows no bounds

no limits and no end.

The type of love I feel

seizes the air in my lungs

bathes me in the downpour

and makes me remember

that I'm still alive.

You leave for the weekend

and in a house all alone

you've left me little hidden notes

with sweet messages

to find in your absence

inside the coffee maker

and in the fridge.

When you're away from me

it's an absence that feels

like an eternity

until you come back to me.

You kissed me as we said goodbye

and another when you return.

You had these walls

around your heart

but, my love,

did you think that

facing that climb

would stop me?

I've completely lost myself

in those twinkling eyes

reflecting the starry night sky

for lying here in the dark

your love is as bright

as a golden sunrise

and I hope this night

will never end.

You like to paint my heart

in shades of your affection

with rich vibrant colors

and dark deepened hues.

My heart is like the autumn

the leaves eventually fall

and you'll be there to paint

my heart in love again.

You take me

higher and higher,

higher than I ever

thought was possible

and even if I survive

such a terrible fall

should we end

I know there are

pieces of me

that would never heal.

I took shelter in your heart

which became a sacred place

with the roots of your soul

steadfast as an ancient oak.

I've never known safety like this

I found living within your heart

with courage now to grow wings

because you've set my spirit free.

I WANT TO BE BY YOUR SIDE

NOT JUST SUNRISE TO SUNSET

BUT FROM SUNRISE TO SUNRISE

AND EVERY DAY AFTER THAT.

The story of our love
is more than just a feeling.
It's a story about navigating
life's biggest challenges
written between moments
of laughter and affection,
a story about how we created
our beautiful world together.

I'm not here

to try to fix you

for when I fell for you

I came to love

all your insecurities,

your perfect little flaws,

because you gave me

a raw type of love

that was able to show me

the deepest essence

of the woman you are.

Spontaneous adventures are

heading down nature trails

having a picnic in a new park

and walking sunset beaches.

Loving you is an adventure

and I can't wait to chase

the next random spot with you.

I never claimed to be perfect

and if you find every flaw in me

that's ok too, for what I want

is to be perfect just for you,

to continue to dance to the

rhythm of our beautiful story

and to wake to another sunrise

with you always by my side.

My goal is to find your heart

among these initial text messages

and a couple nervous dates.

I want to steal your hidden love

so it blooms for no one but me.

Take my hand and follow me

and I will show you a magic

that lights the night on fire

hearts beating with excitement

and two strangers fall in love.

You've created a fire

that burns fierce inside of me.

You've sparked a flame

in which anything is possible.

Sometimes I feel fear

as fire pierces my vulnerability

afraid of the fire

but in love with the flame.

About the Author

As a life-long traveler I've chased love around the world. My goal as a writer is to help readers find that passionate spark that rekindles old emotions or helps ignite a whole new world of feelings. I love the passion that poetry has added to my life, and I hope this book has added a little something extra to your life as well. I would love to hear from you, so feel free to connect with me:

Instagram: @davidwillardwrites

Facebook: @davidwillardwrites

Email: davidwillardwrites@gmail.com

www.ingramcontent.com/pod-product-compliance
Lightning Source LLC
Chambersburg PA
CBHW061820040426
42447CB00012B/2747